THE GOSPEL ACCORDING TO FRANK

poems by

David Lloyd

new american press
Fort Collins, Colo.

new american press

© 2009 by David Lloyd

All rights reserved. No part of this publication may be reproduced, stored in a retrieval system, or transmitted, in any form or by any means, electronic, mechanical, photocopying, recording, or otherwise, without the prior written permission of the copyright holder.

Printed in the United States of America.

ISBN 978-0-9817802-4-5

For ordering information, please contact:

Ingram Book Group
One Ingram Blvd.
La Vergne, TN 37086
(800) 937-8000
orders@ingrambook.com

Certain poems in this book first appeared, sometimes in slightly altered form, in the following magazines:

An Sionnach: A Journal of Literature, Culture, and the Arts; *Bulletin of the Friends of the Owen D. Young and Lauders Libraries*; *Crab Orchard Review*; *Denver Quarterly*; *Great River Review*; *Natural Bridge*; *Planet: the Welsh Internationalist*; and *Stone Canoe*.

*The author wishes to thank the following
for their advice and encouragement:*

John Barnie, David Bowen, Gilbert Gigliotti, Catherine Kasper, Patrick Lawler, Margaret Lloyd, Maureen O'Connor, Julie Olin-Ammentorp, Linda Pennisi, and Kim Waale. He is grateful to the Constance Saltonstall Foundation and the Anderson Center for Interdisciplinary Studies for providing writing residencies, during which many of these poems were written and revised; and to the New York Foundation for the Arts, which provided a Strategic Opportunity Stipend to support publication of this book.

For Kim and Nia

CONTENTS

	Foreword	13
I.	Birth in Hoboken	25
II.	Some Say	26
III.	Yes, Yes, Yes, Yes	27
IV.	The Fight	28
V.	Not I	29
VI.	Creation	30
VII.	The Garden According to Frank	31
VIII.	The Touch	33
IX.	Six Truths About Men and Women	34
X.	Parable of the Knife	36
XI.	The Heavens	37
XII.	Song of Songs (1)	38
XIII.	The Voice	39
XIV.	You Name It, It's Yours	40
XV.	This Way	41
XVI.	The House that Frank Built	43
XVII.	Daydreams	45
XVIII.	Unleashed	46
XIX.	Parable of the Good Samaritans	47
XX.	Uncreation	48
XXI.	Warp-Spasm	49
XXII.	Syllogism	51

XXIII.	Five Proverbs (1)	52
XXIV.	God, and *God*	53
XXV.	Parable of the Hand	54
XXVI.	Song of Songs (2)	55
XXVII.	Parable of the Faithful Servant	56
XXVIII.	A River to His People	58
XXIX.	Song of the Bottle	59
XXX.	Psalm	61
XXXI.	Visiting Bogie	62
XXXII.	Trajectory	63
XXXIII.	Dream at Sunrise	64
XXXIV.	Five Proverbs (2)	65
XXXV.	Reading Emily Dickinson	66
XXXVI.	Parable of the House Built on Sand	67
XXXVII.	Understanding Einstein	68
XXXVIII.	Revelation	69
XXXIX.	Parable of the Prodigal Son	71
XL.	On the Day Gravity Failed	73
XLI.	Six Truths About Money	75
XLII.	Seven Proverbs	77
XLIII.	Frank in His Own Company	79
XLIV.	Retirement	80
XLV.	Still Life in a Park	82
XLVI.	The City According to Frank	83
XLVII.	Eschatology: Frank and Elvis	84
	Notes	87

FOREWORD

In the Company of Frank (and David)

I first became acquainted with the Sinatra poetry of David Lloyd at that seminal moment in "Sinatra Studies," the November 1998 Hofstra University conference, "Frank Sinatra: The Man, The Music, The Legend." Planned well before but held only months after Sinatra's passing, this odd interdisciplinary gathering of scholars and ardent fans juxtaposed academic discourse about and popular memories of Sinatra's remarkable talents, incomparable recordings, iconic images, and inescapable foibles.

The last of these was a sore point for many of the nonacademic attendees: Why the recurrent mention of "mob ties" and other (often alleged) misbehaviors? "All his contemporary performers were singing in the same clubs as he," they'd say, "why aren't they also linked to the likes of Sam Giancana?"

Of course, the stories that surround Sinatra, the true as well as the imagined and the fabricated, privilege Sinatra and argue for a mythic significance for him that all those other performers lack. After all, as good as he was as the featured singer at the Hofstra conference (and as much as Frank loved his voice), there are nonetheless few, if any, great Vic Damone stories. We know Sinatra's so important, however, *because* there are all these tales about him.

And because there are these *poems*, too.

I was quite anxious to meet David at the conclusion of the Hofstra poetry panel, during which he had read one of the selections that would become *The Gospel According to Frank*, first published in 2003. I had been struck that November day, and continue to be, by how his poetry evokes not just Frank Sinatra's life (like his preconcert preparations and intellectual predilections in "The Heavens," and his friendship with Humphrey Bogart in "Visiting Bogie") but also that mythic dimension of the force known as "Sinatra" (like the language of Irish heroic tradition in "Warp-Spasm" and of the Welsh *Mabinogion* in "This Way"). Lloyd's deft coupling of the Hollywood biopic and the traditional epic, of Louella Parsons and Cuchulain, of Marilyn Monroe and the Belle of Amherst (in "Reading Emily Dickinson"), of the profane and the sacred, captures in a wonderfully trenchant but affecting way the aspects of the man/meaning dichotomy that informed my work at that time and the work of many other Sinatra scholars and creative artists ever since.

For "Sinatra Studies" has flourished since that conference in 1998, as a January 2009 article in *The Chronicle Review* of *The Chronicle of Higher Education* made clear. Since a good introduction to an excellent poetry sequence is rarely a review of scholarly literature, I will only mention that such well-documented and intensely-focused studies like *Sessions with Sinatra: Frank Sinatra and the Art of Recording* by Charles Granata (1999), *Frank Sinatra: History, Identity, and Italian American Culture*, edited by Stanislao G. Pugliese (2004), and Karen McNally's *When Frankie Went to Hollywood: Frank Sinatra and American Male Identity* (2008) — not to mention my *A Storied Singer: Frank Sinatra as Literary Conceit* (2002), Summers and Swan's much-ballyhooed *Sinatra The Life* (2005), and Tom Santopietro's *Sinatra in Hollywood* (2008) — show that, even as time passes, Sinatra's importance as a cultural figure has not and need not wane.

This fine work builds upon that begun before Hofstra, of course: the archival work of Lonstein and Marino's *The Revised Complete Sinatra* (1979), supplemented by Tom Rednour's excellent, if terribly-subtitled, *Songs by Sinatra: A Unique Frank Sinatra Songography* (1998); the unequaled biography of Will Friedwald, *Sinatra: The Song is You: A Singer's Art* (1995); Leonard Mustazza's collection *Frank Sinatra and Popular Culture: Essays on an American Icon* (1998); *The Frank Sinatra Reader*, edited by Steven Petkov and Mustazza (1997); Bill Zehme's entertaining *The Way You Wear Your Hat: Frank Sinatra and the Lost Art of Livin'* (1997); and the ultimate Sinatra vade mecum, Pete Hamill's *Why Sinatra Matters* (1998).

The Sinatra children have weighed in, as well: Nancy with *Frank Sinatra: My Father* (1986) and the helpful chronology of *Frank Sinatra: An American Legend* (1998); Tina with *The Man and His Art* (1991) and *My Father's Daughter* (2000); and, perhaps most insightful of all, Frank Jr.'s compact disc of musical appreciation and memoir, *As I Remember It*, released by Angel Records (1996) with, for example, its step-by-step unpacking of Nelson Riddle's 1956 Capitol Records arrangement of "Lonesome Road" from *A Swingin' Affair*. While clearly sources that need scrutiny before use as evidence, they offer personal and even professional insights that scholars should examine and from which we all can learn.

More to the point here, perhaps, creative writers of all genres—songwriters, playwrights, novelists, and poets—have continued to find in Sinatra (and the songs, films, legends, and people with whom he is tied) an inexhaustible source of inspiration. Frank was first mentioned by name in a 1945 song introduced by the Benny Goodman Orchestra, "This and That," and continues to inspire music from every musical category (rap, folk, metal, country, jazz, emo, pop, alternative, and, if we include Nancy, even classical). Sinatra also has inspired such plays as *Lamppost Reunion* by Louis Russo II (1975), *Playing Sinatra* by Bernard Kops (1992), and *"If It Was Easy..."* by Stewart Lane and Ward Morehouse III (2002), as well as a forthcoming Broadway adaptation of the 1964 Rat Pack musical film *Robin and the Seven Hoods*. Novelists like the Spaniard Raul Nuñez (*Sinatra*, 1984), Michael Ventura (*The Death of Frank Sinatra*, 1996), Don DeLillo (the "Pafko at the Wall" novella adapted from *Underworld*, 1997), Sam Kashner (*Sinatraland*, 1999), Max Allan Collins (*Chicago Confidential*, 2003), David Ohle (*The Age of Sinatra*, 2004), and Robert J. Randisi (a series of "Rat Pack Mysteries"), all find in Sinatra, his times, and his circle a rich tapestry of personal conflict, socio-political commentary, and some good murder plots.

For poets, here are just a few names, other than David Lloyd, from my 2008 anthology *Sinatra: But Buddy I'm a Kind of Poem*: Allen Ginsberg, Kathleen Norris, Virgil Suarez, Robert Wrigley, Ruth Stone, Jill Bialosky, Landis Everson, Beckian Fritz Goldberg, David Lehman, Ravi Shankar, Maria Mazziotti Gillan, Paul Fericano, Emily XYZ, and Jeremy Reed. While each of these poets and performers mines a particular Sinatra vein (his music, fame, struggles, politics—both liberal and conservative—heritage, toughness, ubiquity, love, family, nostalgia, anger, tenderness, etc.), no one had before, or since, attempted such a wide-ranging and sustained grappling with a poetic Sinatra as David Lloyd in *The Gospel According to Frank*.

And, spread the good news, it's now new and improved!

In *A Storied Singer*, I had the pleasure of writing about the depiction of Sinatra in "The Heavens," the poem that David had presented at Hofstra. It reads, in part:

> *An artist who apparently senses the right questions to consider but who cannot resolve them successfully, Lloyd's Sinatra, in the end, is himself at risk in the neon-lit desert. He alone may make the effort to "lean further out and squint" at the stars in the sky, but it is his, as much as the Earth's, presence that casts such an imposing shadow and blots them out. Incapable of*

> *breaking free from the world he has helped to create, Sinatra, both moth and flame, cannot but abandon his quest or risk destroying himself in the process. As the poem suggests in the shrug of the singer's shoulders and his habitual gestures of straightening his tie and checking the time, his choice is sadly clear. When the Copa is waiting downstairs, the heavens can wait.*

This already loaded depiction of Sinatra is only enriched throughout the rest of the book with images and language drawn from Sinatra's life, the Bible, and traditional Celtic and classical literature.

The reader can glean truths of Sinatra's life, loves, and career here (Ava, Dino, Sammy, Peter, Elvis, JFK, the retirement, the power Frank had and the powers he did not), but that's never the sole focus. From the book's (and Frank's) beginnings, the poems intentionally blur the line between the individual life and its larger (-than-life) significances, between reality and tall tale, between *historia* and *mythopoeisis*. In "Birth in Hoboken," for example, we encounter the "legend" of Sinatra's difficult birth and ponder his wish not to be born but to stay in "endless and splendid isolation...always suspended, always playtime." The poem challenges us to think that, perhaps, Sinatra at many points in his real life lived just that way, but with "his first note cracking / every window and mirror in Hoboken," we also know that achieving that summit of ease (and loneliness) won't be easy.

In "On the Day Gravity Failed," Frank simply starts floating upward. He asks himself:

> ...why not? why not?
> why not *fly up and away*
> by flapping arms, kicking legs,
> accepting the miracle
> not for any flying honeymoon
> but alone and silent and unrepentant

But, "not seeing the odds / in his favor," he rejects the chance and returns to earth with "a sigh of relief" to face again the crowd, that same crowd that doesn't, and indeed cannot, understand him. Miracles happen "without...consent," but we don't always take full advantage and often find such opportunities inconvenient. Frank flew often, the poem suggests, but he perhaps only rarely soared.

While some passages cannot but cause a smile (e.g., the creator's feet hanging "a good ways / over the edge" of "a bed as big as the sky" in "Creation"), Lloyd never separates such whimsy from how:

> ...he created Eve
> from the rib of a nameless man
> who suffered horribly
> and died soon after. She was distant,
> faithless, and without hope.

For, although at poem's end this Paradise may be declared "the life," it can never be achieved cheaply. And so this interlocking nature of life's joy and sorrow, of its pleasure and pain, of its love and hurt, pervades the poems as it did Sinatra's life. Consider the fourth of "Seven Proverbs":

> Profuse are the kisses of a friend
> but faithful
> are the wounds of an enemy.

If the pain of battle is truer than the affections of loved ones, and even love hurts, then whom should one really embrace? Time and again, we see Lloyd's Sinatra and, consequently, ourselves faced with this question.

The revised edition offers some minor reordering and, more significantly, several new poems, including "Song of Songs" 1 and 2 and "Psalms," that punctuate the sequence and further emphasize the scriptural theme. The first two, in the erotic tradition of King David's poetry, treat the beauty and intensity of love. In each, however, is also revealed the lethal narcissism that lurks within every relationship. Other new poems, like "Still Life in a Park" and "Trajectory," illustrate further the almost cosmic pull of this selfishness:

> *Oh to be young! –*
> *and not give a shit about you*
>
> *or your friend*
> *or the person next to your friend...*

and

> *We organized the universe into orbit*
> *around ourselves...*

While we all harbor such hurtful tendencies, luckily few of us have the clout to shape reality to our whims. Lloyd's Sinatra offers readers a chance to ponder the fallout from just such power.

The most exciting of the new poems for me is "Frank in His Own Company," the title of which echoes a line from the 1940 Dorsey/Sinatra collaboration "We Three (My Echo, My Shadow, and Me)" and which depicts Frank's looking at himself in funhouse mirrors:

> *...remorseless light, silence,*
> *the isolated self, replicated –*
> *in case you don't get it the first time –*
> *a thousand thousand times:*
> *an army of Frank diminished*
> *to a speck at the back*
> *of the endless single file*

This sense of Frank's being surrounded by nothing but himself emphasizes the loneliness that all the biographies stress—his always feeling alone whether it's in a room full of friends or in a concert hall full of listeners.

The poem also elicits comparisons to the carny setting of Gerald Early's "Listening to Frank Sinatra," in which a father recounts a tale from his youth about hearing a sideshow attraction confess that he spends his days listening to Sinatra. For this reason, the father forever seeks to hear the singer's voice wherever he goes (much to his children's dismay). In Lloyd's poem, Frank is at the carny—indeed thousands of him are there—but in some ways he's even more trapped than the sideshow attraction was—for he has only his own company to keep.

The good news for readers is that, in *The Gospel According to Frank*, David Lloyd offers us a Sinatra portrait that yields a multitude of pleasures and meanings, always worth the time and never easy. As he describes in "The City According to Frank," here are:

> ...those open spaces, the infinite
> possibilities, the uncomfortable green,
> the still-breathing leaves.

Spend some time in the company of David's Frank; he's good company indeed.

Gilbert L. Gigliotti
Central Connecticut State University

---

[i] I will leave it to individual readers and geneticists to decide the merit of Julie Sinatra's claims in *Under My Skin: Frank Sinatra, My Father The Man Behind the Mystique* (2007).

[ii] Cf. Michael Daughtery's "Sinatra Shag" (1997) and Thomas Ades' "Jatekok (Playing Games): *"Hommage a* Nancy Sinatra" (2000).

[iii] One might argue that the Rod McKuen songs and poems that comprise the 1969 album *A Man Alone* written specifically for, and recorded by, Sinatra are the first to treat Sinatra so fully, but, as I argue in *A Storied Singer*, if we acknowledge anyone outside of the man himself with the creation of the Sinatra character, then the credit goes to his longtime songwriter and friend Sammy Cahn.

[iv] Only Greg Rappleye's "Last Walk with Sinatra's Dog" (2000) and "From the Vegas *Cantos*" (1999) and Matt Santateresa's "Frank Sinatra, Drunk, Turns His Gunsights on a Dolphin off Corsica," offer a similar approach: narrative poetry with decidedly mythic overtones. "Last Walk" is based on Homer's *Odyssey* XI.138-157; "*Cantos*" offers an epic take on a road trip to the desert by the cast of *Ocean's 11* to watch a nuclear test, and "Dolphin" depicts a Sinatra at his uninhibited worst.

My kind of crazy world . . .

from "Why Try to Change Me Now?"
recorded by Frank Sinatra
17 September 1952
New York, NY

I. BIRTH IN HOBOKEN

Because he was so huge
they pulled him out with forceps
long as pool cues, half-killing
the almost-forgotten mother.

But afterwards, as he lay on the table
by the bloodied tools, he wouldn't open his eyes,
wouldn't leave his dream
of endless and splendid isolation,
always ninety eight point six,
always suspended, always playtime.

It took a waterfall to wake him,
his first note cracking every
window and mirror in Hoboken.

And why not?
Why should he wish to leave
the amniotic slumber for a childhood
of boxing gyms, scrap-heaps, doughboys,
and soon-to-leap stock brokers
so much unlike himself?

Every legend needs a legend
from which the hero rises like a flame
from a greasy stove, like a mushroom
from manure, like a song
from the lips of a kid on a street corner
whose partner strums a ukulele.

II. SOME SAY . . .

(1)

Some say he was born out of his father's head
and afterwards ate that head
and threw up a new interpretation of himself:
smarter, more talented, free of scars.

That self refused to remember
what came before
when passing him on the street
or in a house or in a mirror.

(2)

Some say his father's head
threw him up as an afterthought
but foolishly rolled away

from what lay steaming on the ground,
unable to rise on unsteady legs –
but rising nonetheless.

(3)

Some say that when he was born
his father picked him up and pressed
the small forehead against his own large forehead.

Afterwards, neither could remember the moment,
even when passing each other on the street
or in a house or when speaking of the hall of mirrors
that is the distant past.

III. YES, YES, YES, YES

No, he didn't have much.

Yes, he grew up in a tough neighborhood,
the skyscrapers and high rises across the river
eclipsing the sun and moon from his streets.

And yes he played stickball in those blacked-out alleys
among garbage cans everyone filled
but only the rats thought to empty.

And yes the sticks he used were the torn off legs
of his boyhood enemies. And yes their severed heads
were the balls. And yes he could always hit those
further and harder than any playmate,
busting through the brick, metal and mortar

of the alley walls, curving over the river to the city
and up and up and up like the first ever sputnik
to smash a window of a CEO's office
on the one hundred and twelfth floor. "It's OK, it's OK,"

the CEO shouted, waving at Frank and leaning out
through the space his window had filled.
"That's quite the swing for a skinny kid."

But these are old stories,
the ones everyone knows, the ones
we tell our children's children, the stories
about which even his grandparents would say,

"Yes, yes, yes, yes.
But tell us something we don't know."

IV. THE FIGHT

One day you will fight,
his father explained at bedtime.

Not because you want to.
Not because you have anything to gain.
Not because anyone asks you to.
Not because you are defending a coin
at the bottom of your pocket.

You will fight because weapons held too long
feel more like hands
than your own hands ever looked or felt.

And they will always be ready.

V. NOT I

It was Frank who grew the famous tree,
sprouting it from his own rib, untimely ripped.

It was Frank also who ate the fruit of the tree,
enticing himself with beauties beyond good and evil.

He consumed not just the bruised skin, seeds, and core of one,
but all the fruit in the forest,

then chopped and burned the trees
in the first bonfire of the first summer

of the first turning of the earth.
Afterwards, he hid from himself and sang,

a capello, his first hit: *It was not I, not I,
not I*, hypnotizing himself

with those words until the end of time –
though there was always, deep in his apple soul,

that difficult-to-assassinate doubt,
the one that caused him

to exile himself from himself and from those others
in the Garden spending their lives in the hunt

for the trees and the apples
but finding only ashes at the end

of a well-trodden path.

VI. CREATION

On the first day he created radio.
On the second day, *My Way*.
On the third day, *From Here to Eternity*.
On the fourth, Dino, Sammy, Peter,
with personalities and scripts.

And on the fifth day, he created Eve
from the rib of a nameless man
who suffered horribly
and died soon after. She was distant,
faithless, and without hope.

And on the sixth day he saw that it was good.

And he rested on the seventh day with Eve,
a cigarette, and a bottle of Jack Daniels
in a bed as big as the sky –
and still his feet hung a good ways
over the edge.

This right here, he shouted,
toasting himself and his appetites
as Eve dreamed of Adam.
This here is the life.

VII. THE GARDEN ACCORDING TO FRANK

There's no good or evil separate
from what his mind imagines.

The fruit of the tree, for example,
bestows not knowledge but forgetfulness.
The serpent whispers its secret
to gossip columnists, who promise
to name their source.

A thousand chorus girls parade their smiles
and platters of iced shrimp.
A thousand illegal immigrants maintain
the continent-sized golf course,
restricted to a membership of one.

Adam skulks at a distance –
out of sight, out of mind.

Cain murders Abel each night,
and each morning bloodied Abel rises
to be killed again.
You're a good kid, Frank tells him,
slapping a fifty into his limp hand.

Their descendents will build a city
with foundations in the sand,
whose towers invade the heavens,
whose spotlights discover planets,
whose machines swallow fortunes,
whose billboards proclaim
A Place in the Sun
and every product that money can invent.

* * *

All right. Frank announces at a microphone plugged into the center of the universe.

Let the games begin.

VIII. THE TOUCH

His father touched him
and the boy remembered
and promised to pass it on
to his own child, if he could find his way.

Though it burned like a brand,
the boy was proud of its making
and later, in his most intimate moments,
would reveal the scar

as if to say, *See, here is something
no one else has felt or will feel.
You may touch it.
But you will never understand it.*

IX. SIX TRUTHS ABOUT MEN AND WOMEN

(1)

In truth, there was no dust, no rib, no apple.
She created him
as much as he created her,
endowing his form with her fears and illusions,
believing that this way
she might free herself from herself.

(2)

In truth, they created themselves
each in the other's likeness
that they might never be alone,
shaping faces, knitting bones
from their imperfect understandings
of each other's faults and perfections.

(3)

In truth, it wasn't infidelity
but indifference that betrayed them
in the days before the arguments
and the exile
and the distance
and the regret
and everything that occurred thereafter.

(4)

In truth, how they loved each other!
Loving because of what they loved
in themselves shining out
from the other's averted face.

(5)

In truth, she created the Garden
after she ate the apple
and invited him to join her
because she knew he would walk through
the delightful shapes and fragrances
as if he owned them.

(6)

In truth, there are many truths
about who they were together,
who they might have been
and might yet be, staring
at each other's beautiful forms,
scooping up handfuls
of the dust around their feet.

X. PARABLE OF THE KNIFE

When Abraham raised his knife,
the knife itself became the God of the Garden,

content to take a life
or leave it.

The knife hung in the air
as still as a moon.

It sliced the setting sun
like an angry prism.

It was close by
and it was remote.

Self-contained in its earthly vessel,
the knife didn't recognize

the hand that held it, didn't hear
the boy whimpering beneath.

Above, invisible planets slowly turned
around their epicenter,

remembering their origins
as only planets can remember.

The knife cared,
and it didn't care at all.

XI. THE HEAVENS

All the moths of Nevada seek out
these infamous lights, immolating themselves
in countless sparks on the "S" and the "d"
of the Sands Hotel.

With all the shuffling, rolling, clanking
money machines, the infinite décolletage
and spinning ice cubes, the smoke
and the mirrors, no one sees
this dusty descent of bodies and wings,
antennae and legs, the steady yearning,
the tiny deaths that don't stop.

No one sees, that is, but Frank,
staring up from the balcony of his three-bedroom,
second-floor suite, cigarette poised between fingers,
a Jack Daniels on the rocks with a twist
and a swizzle at the ready.
Where do they come from? he asks,
as if a flunky with an answer was waiting.
Why, he wants to know, *don't they stop?*

Frank leans further out and squints.
But no stars dot this desert sky. No meteors
beginning somewhere, ending elsewhere.
No revelations beyond what revolving numbers can tell.
Here, the earth casts its brilliant shadow
over all the heavens, everywhere and forever.

Frank shrugs his shoulders,
checks his watch, tightens the knot
of his tie, flicks a half-inch of ash
over the railing for the desert breeze to dissect.
Downstairs, the Copa waits.

XII. SONG OF SONGS (1)

Some day, the father said,
*a woman will reach into your rib cage
and curl her fingers around your beating heart.*
Will it hurt? the boy asked.
Exquisitely, the father replied.
And will she let go? the boy asked.
Sometimes, the father said, *if you are unlucky.*

*But other times she'll squeeze and squeeze
until the heart is as small and cold as a diamond
embedded in a rock. And she will set that diamond
upon an altar and worship it
as if it wasn't a thing she made.*

And is that all? the boy wanted to know.
The father drew in a breath so deep
it touched his fingernails. *Other times,* he said,
*she will hold the heart like the petal of a flower
that blooms once in a lifetime.*
And then it is possible, he continued,
that she will never let go.

XIII. THE VOICE

You can't have the song without the bird,
the voice without the body.

How did this happen? one asked.
It is soon told:

>   Naked, mute, without hunger or thirst,
>   the body lay on the ground,
>   contemplating during a night that lasted decades
>   the fresh layers of stars, constellations, galaxies.
>
>   So infinitesimal in their presence,
>   the body had nothing to say.
>   It felt no urge to expel its thoughts
>   but allowed them to swim in the mind
>   as in a bottomless ocean.
>
>   A serpent chanced by
>   and seeing the body at rest,
>   dripped into its ear all the sounds
>   stolen over many lifetimes,
>   and slipped away.
>
>   The body felt a needle of hunger,
>   a throat on fire with thirst,
>   legs and arms cramped
>   from lying so still, so long.
>
>   It closed its eyes, opened its lips.
>   And through the lips, the voice was born:
>   delicate, perfectly pitched.
>   "Me," it sang. And again:
>   "Me, Me, Me."

XIV. YOU NAME IT, IT'S YOURS

When at the end of her all night lap dance
Salomie asked for the head
of a certain tabloid critic on a cold cut platter,
Frank hesitated.

That's it? he finally shouted
so loudly every eardrum on earth popped.
Only his head? And only a platter?

*Why should the head of his wife
remain attached?
Doesn't he have children as yet unharmed?*

*How about a flood to submerge his species?
Or a retrovirus whose antidote is annihilation?
Or a supernova in his soup?*

*Or the universe in a reverse big bang,
crushing him and all reality
to an incomprehensively dense pinprick
that not even I can find?*

Just tell me what you want, Frank insisted
from his cushioned throne.
You name it, it's yours.

But Salomie was a young girl, inexperienced
in the take and give of Frank's world.
Just his head, she repeated.
*On a cold cut platter.
That'll do it.*

XV. THIS WAY

"Will you, for God's sake and for my sake, tell me how you might be killed? Since my memory is better as a safeguard than yours."
"I will gladly tell," he said.

– from the Fourth Branch of *The Mabinogi*

It's not easy, Frank told Ava as they lay in bed
after too many drinks loosed his tongue,

even though she never asked,
even though she never cared. *Only this way,*

Frank explained: *Only if when preparing
for my Sunday bath Sammy, Dino, Joey and Peter*

*follow me in and strip off my tuxedo then lift me
so that one foot rests on the head of a crouching*

*Bing Crosby and one on the rim of my gold-plated bathtub,
steaming with freshly-drawn water;*

*and only then if a handsome actor from Spain rushes out
of the bathroom closet waving a knife he has honed*

*and polished every Sunday for a year,
and only then if that year is the forty-third year*

*of my life, and only then if the handsome actor
releases my heart from its duties*

*with three quick stabs and offers it, still-beating,
to the one I love most while Bing nonchalantly*

*   *   *

*considers the horror above him and my legs quake
and my feet forget their balance and their blood.*

Only then, mused Frank, *only then will I be truly killed
rather than deeply and endlessly wounded.*

All right, said Ava with a bored smile
as she reached for her drink on the night stand.

I'll see what I can do.

XVI. THE HOUSE THAT FRANK BUILT

Frank spent one of his fortunes
on an architectural impossibility made of glass,
with glass appliances, glass furniture, glass bedsheets,
glass glasses, glass guns.

On his first day inside, Frank looked down
at the world stretching beneath his bedroom,
and focused on a friend
behaving as badly as he'd forgotten he'd behaved
the night before with a woman
whose name he'd misplaced.

Enraged, he plunged a thumb
through the house and into the earth
to pluck out a stone that he hurled at his friend,
dividing the head from the body so cleanly
the body continued its bad habits for three more days
before understanding its end had come and gone.

The liberated head rolled according to prevailing winds,
frightening children, telling stories that didn't matter
to anyone who'd listen
until it gathered speed and altitude, increased mass,
traced the curve of the earth, shaved the tops of forests,
skipped across great lakes, pierced the highest ocean waves
and proved the earth to be as round as a bodiless head
by arriving back to its origin and entering
the house that Frank built,
smashing it to dangerous diamonds
before settling like a pet
behind his newly polished shoes.

* * *

God damn it! Frank shouted at the house that was,
at the still-talking head, at the cowering earth,
at the heavens that remained speechless
because nothing was more important than themselves.

God damn it! he shouted again.
God damn it all to hell!

XVII. DAYDREAMS

That was always the trick:
to make the daydream more real than reality.

With Frank, just the lift of an eyebrow
in the hotel lobby, and a cigarette appears,

held out by a girl with strap and tray,
bellboy cap, bright ironic smile.

She lights him up. He winks,
tucks a bill beneath her strap.

He sucks the smoke so deeply
the cigarette disappears.

Then he fills the lobby with his slow exhale,
a breath so dense no one can see

the ash drift down, or the doors, elevators,
registration desk, exit lights,

or one another's faces, or their feet
as they wander,

eyes squinting, hands held out
as if to keep someone or some thing at bay.

XVIII. UNLEASHED

On the field of battle, Frank played dirty,
unleashing from his armed Underworld
the dogs that don't go away:

>the Dog of the Dark Glasses,
>the Dog of the Dollar Held Back,
>the Dog of the Dreadful Scowl,
>the Dog of Gigantic Generosity,
>the Dog of the Erect Penis Close By,
>the Dog of the Erect Penis Distant,
>the Dog of Sentimental Worship of the Mother,
>the Dog of Never Forgetting,
>the Dog of the Easy Smile,
>and the terrible, terrible Dog of *Who Cares?*

Slap him, Frank ordered the waiter,
pointing at the restaurant table
where his old enemy sat and ate.

*Slap his face. Slap him hard,
or else you're history.*

And the waiter shuffled over,
raised his hand, closed his eyes,
swung his arm with all his strength
and felt himself shrink.

Frank nodded and smiled.
He tipped the waiter profoundly
just before the diminished nobody
disappeared from sight.

XIX. PARABLE OF THE GOOD SAMARITANS

A man seeking his fortune in the city was attacked by robbers who beat him, stripped him, left him for dead at the roadside under an unfriendly sun.

A priest traveling that road found him, blessed him, gave him the shoes from his feet, and continued on his way.

A judge in a limousine rolled down his window, tossing the man the shirt off his back before speeding to a session at court.

A politician in a helicopter dropped him a sandwich and a hat before reversing his binoculars to make the man disappear.

From the sandwich, he gained strength to lick his wounds. He stripped fur from a roadside carcass to bind where the blood flowed. He staggered to the nearest house, where he stole food and drink from a family that had little of their own.

That night he slept in a broken barn among the poor and the ill and the homeless, who fell upon him before dawn, stealing the food he'd stolen, stripping off even his bloodied bandages, beating him because of the priest's shoes, the judge's shirt, the politician's hat.

And they rolled him into a ditch where he died, naked and alone, crying out his anger to the silent heavens, yet still dreaming, still dreaming of the city and the fortune that should have been his for the taking.

XX. UNCREATION

Like the hand of a long-dead friend,
a starling alights on Frank's vast shoulder
with news of its travels over many decades
through the dangerous world:

a naked girl running from napalm,
famine in North Africa,
Eisenhower asleep,
the universe rushing away from itself,
cornfields sown with silos –

until with a thumb and a finger
Frank reaches over
and shuts its beak. *What the hell!*
Frank yells, fixing the bird's terrified eye
with his own steely blue.
I don't remember making you.

And the starling, confronted
with its unreality,
abruptly disappears.

XXI. WARP-SPASM

One night Peter met Ava for drinks at the Luau
where someone saw them being seen

by everyone who's anyone, except Frank,
and the someone told Louella Parsons,

who told her readers who told each other
news already old the next morning.

Where's Frank in all of this? Frank asked himself,
so sorry at the death of love, the insubstantial treason,

the post-mortum of an illusion once world-renowned.
But rage, rage, thank God, is its own reward,

before, during, and after; that pulse of life
coiled like a vicious jack-in-the-box,

its lid perpetually about to pop
and release into the world the screaming head.

It takes a lifetime of practice to get it right.
It takes a self large as a skyscraper.

Muscles tense, brow furrows, teeth grind,
testicles swell ten times their size, pores leak,

eyes swivel in their sockets, hairs like bayonets,
bourbon sucked down by the quart.

Ready, at last. Two in the morning
on the phone to Peter: *What the fuck*

* * *

you doing with Ava?
You want both your legs broken?

Rage and release. Rage and release.
So good to be alive.

XXII. SYLLOGISM

When money pumps out
from the rows of flashing machines
and the barman's top shelf glitters
wall to wall, ceiling to floor;
and everyone in every room
in the only building that matters
is young, or thinks he's young,
or acts like he's young,
or pays good money to be near the young;
and style is a moment
on a downward spiral no one sees
but all respect;

then, there's no reason
to search out a window or a clock
or a hidden corner to sit in,
alone, cross-legged,
your head in your hands
and your mouth shut tight.

XXIII. FIVE PROVERBS (1)

(1)

He who stuffs a camel through the needle's eye
without assessing the damage
impresses even a God.

(2)

He who choreographs the angels
on the head of a pin
need not worry about their number.

(3)

He who adorns himself
like one of the lilies of the field
or like a sparrow fallen from a tree
will forever keep God's attention.

(4)

He who loves himself, spares the rod;
he who hates himself
is diligent with discipline.

(5)

A false witness may go unpunished,
but he who tells the truth risks calamity.

XXIV. GOD, AND *GOD*

There's power, Frank had to admit
if only to himself,
and then there's *power*. Which is what
Jack Kennedy taught him during their minutes
of imagined intimacy, his finger always poised
a half inch above a heavily-guarded button
no matter where his eyes might dart.

Press it, and men drown in the Bay of Pigs.
Press again, a woman falls to the pavement in Saigon.
Again, and a man gasps
in Baghdad. One last time, and, and ...

Frank never found such a button,
despite years of searching,
though he knew its shape and color,
though he called himself a friend
to some of the men who owned
the most important fingers.

XXV. PARABLE OF THE HAND

Science tells us
that at the right temperature
a hand will freeze,

at another it will burn,
at yet another,

feel nothing or feel pain
or evaporate to bone

or want nothing or cease
to exist or exist forever

or desire forever, stretching
at the right temperature

towards the nearest thing
that can't be touched.

XXVI. SONG OF SONGS (2)

Some day, the father said,
*you will reach in through a rib cage
and curl your fingers
around the beating heart of a woman.*
And will it hurt? the boy asked.
Exquisitely, the father replied.
And will I let go? the boy asked.
Perhaps, the father said, *if you are unlucky.*

*But other times you will squeeze and squeeze
until the heart is malleable as clay.
And you will form that lump
into a little statue of yourself.*

And is that all? the boy wanted to know.
The father drew in a breath so deep
it lifted the hair from his head.
Other times, he said, *you will make of that lump
a form never before seen.*
And it is possible, he continued,
that you will never let go.

XXVII. PARABLE OF THE FAITHFUL SERVANT

A man preparing for a journey entrusted his wealth to his servants. To one he gave five thousand dollars, to another, two thousand, to a third, a thousand, each according to his talent.

The one with five thousand invested it and made five more, three of which he kept for himself. The one with two thousand invested that, making two thousand more, half of which he kept.

But he who received the one thousand buried it in his master's garden, where he watered it and guarded it night and day.

In the spring, what he buried sprouted into a tree. And its fruit were golden apples, a hundred to each branch.

When men hearing of the tree journeyed from great distances to worship at its roots, he beat them back, then enclosed the garden with a wall mounted with spikes and razors.

But still the worshippers came, gathering in a pauper's village where they murmured prayers, wept, brought forth the lame, the leprous, the blind, held up old pots, believing that a gust of wind might toss an apple.

One night the one who guarded the tree crept into the rooms of his fellow servants, cut their throats, stole their money, and buried one each side of the tree so their flesh would nourish its growth.

* * *

When the master returned, he rejoiced when his least able servant brought him to the tree and its fruit.

"I will set you above all others in my house," he said. But it was the servant who had planted the tree, guarded it, loved it as no other. He had murdered men so the tree could thrive. Weren't the golden apples tinged with red?

His master set guards and dogs against him. And because the servant had no home, he lived outside the wall with the other worshippers, murmuring poisonous prayers night and day in the hope that the tree might wither, its fruit shrivel, and the wrong done be avenged.

XXVIII. A RIVER TO HIS PEOPLE

The drink is a beautiful thing,
transparent yet mimicking, in its absolute circle,
the barroom's fixtures, fingers, rings, faces;

shimmering from the purr and the bark,
from the voices projecting themselves
onto all available screens.

It moves the imagination to see
in four disappearing cubes, all limbs
and postures desired and contained
and released.

Heavier than you'd think, indestructible,
snug and comfortable as a hand held by a hand
that knows its business.

Another round on me, Frank shouts
to the bartender
who can never go home.

And out from his pocket he pulls
in one huge fist
all the dollars in the world.

XXIX. SONG OF THE BOTTLE

The bottle tells stories
about the stories that happened
and stories about the stories that didn't happen
to distract from the ones that did.

So sensitive, the bottle feels
the slightest breath or brush of lips
on its glassy, labeled skin,
though everything dripped upon it
slides to a dark pool.

As its answer to the noise of others
and the noise corked inside,
the bottle has perfected a crouched
and hungry silence.
At the same time, it talks, constantly,
reaching out because of the difficulty
of going in.

Sometimes on a cool summer evening,
when birds and bats are roused
by the sun's absence and a rising breeze,
the bottle weeps, silently,
with tears drawn from the air.
So sad, that cool summer evening.
So sad those birds and bats.

To keep from falling asleep,
the bottle sings the oldest of old
drinker's songs: the one about the Self,
its frenzied frolics, its Selfness,
the Self's adventures at the center of the Self,
its worries about the Self, its fearful fragility,

its always half-emptiness, its viscous guilt,
magnified and diminished and magnified
by the bartender's obliging mirrors.
So sad, so sad, the song
of the bottled, billowed Self.

The bottle sings and sings
to keep from falling asleep.
Once asleep, it never wakes.
It never wakes up.

XXX. PSALM

Three things God asked of me:
my love, my prayers, my loyalty.

These I hung upon the branches
of an oak tree

that grew and spread
until the three

were at last free of me:
my love, my prayers, my loyalty.

XXXI. VISITING BOGIE

Sammy clowned.

Dino mixed martinis.

Peter pinched the nurse's bottom

and swore it was Joey

who swore it was Sammy

who swore it was Peter,

who picked up and drained Dino's martini

and demanded another.

"How's your bird?" Frank asked,

but Bogie, propped on pillows,

couldn't answer

because of the cancer eating his throat

and his eyes rolling in his head.

XXXII. TRAJECTORY

We stood from the ground.

We stretched arms into air.

We climbed above the canopy.

We laid stones upon stones upon stones.

We hauled ourselves up the highest mountain,
littering trails with our sherpas.

We constructed skyscrapers
that only we could topple.

We improved upon birds.

We saw everything that we were not.

We expanded ourselves to a mass
greater than the greatest planet.

We burned hotter than our sun
and more distantly.

We organized the universe into orbit
around ourselves, then sucked into our belly

all near objects so insistently
not one can remember

if it ever had a body of its own.

XXXIII. DREAM AT SUNRISE

The sun rises over route 91,
over unblossomed flowers, solitary rocks,
sharkskin suits buried
with their bodies in the sand.

It causes shards from smashed bottles to shine.
It seeks out the hotel billboard,
inspects the blinds,
locates a crack, creeps up the bed
to bathe in light the famous face
dreaming of Hoboken, Uncle Babe, Champ Sieger,
those prelapsarian days.

His eyelids creak open,
his hand fumbles for the nearest shot glass
and hurls it through space,
shattering the sun to cinders
on the carpet of the darkened room.
Outside: planets bereft of light.

Frank groans, rolls over,
and enters his dream again.

XXXIV. FIVE PROVERBS (2)

(1)

Do not trust your children
because it is from you that they learn
the wisdom of the world.

(2)

Let your own mouth and not another's
praise your deeds,
for a soft tongue will break a bone.

(3)

Despise your parents when they are old
for you may be sure
they once despised you.

(4)

Stolen water is sweet,
and bread eaten in secret is pleasant,
for it is the glory of God to conceal things.

(5)

Rejoice when your enemy falls,
let your heart be glad when he stumbles,
for the Lord sees all things
and never forgets.

XXXV. READING EMILY DICKINSON

In Arthur and Marilyn's living room,
Frank's bored with his drink, his bowl of cashews,
the shouting from the kitchen.
It's going to be a long night.

He glances around, checks out a painting
that he never understood,
scans the books under the coffee table,
picks one up, opens it:

"Tell all the Truth but tell it slant – Success …"
Then, "My Life had stood – a Loaded Gun – "
and then, "Vesuvius – at Home."

More shouts from the kitchen. A glass breaks.

Not bad, he thinks, and continues:
"Zero at the Bone" and
"I heard a Fly buzz when I died"
just as Marilyn pops her head – then herself –
around the door,

mascara smudged, martini swirling,
its olive a world dislodged from orbit.
Her lips await the next kiss.

Who cares? Frank thinks, shutting the book.
Not me.

Arthur's a no-show, sitting at the kitchen table,
his face firmly in his hands.

XXXVI. PARABLE OF THE HOUSE BUILT ON SAND

A rich man ordered his sons each to build a house. The most able would gain his inheritance.

The first built a house on rock, the second on the plain, the third on a shining hill.

And a fault opened and swallowed the house on rock, grinding it between ancient jaws.

And damp entered the house on the plain, rotting its beams and floorboards until a flood carried the shreds away.

And windstorms battered the house on the shining hill until it slid into the valley, where scavengers stole the remnants for their dark hovels.

But the father had spent his fortune in secret building on sand a house as unmanageable as a city. The house proved strong and dry. It bore fruit and multiplied into a mirage of houses that disappeared and reappeared with each hot breeze.

And men hearing of this miracle enslaved other men to cut roads into the wilderness and over mountains and through foreign nations to seize it from the one who built it.

They drained the heavens to water the city. They killed every creeping creature and every flying one for food. They sacrificed their families to gain dominion over that distant place.

XXXVII. UNDERSTANDING EINSTEIN

Frank didn't want to know
that theory about time bending like a bad back.

He didn't want to know that a man
trapped in a plane forever circling the earth

cannot die. Or that the briefest distance
between birth and death

leads through a back alley in Hoboken.
Or that two bodies orbiting elliptically

can never touch. Or that Las Vegas
will rediscover its emptiness

when the apocalyptic payloads
blast off from Sodom and Gomorrah.

But some things must always be true,
Frank insisted, in desperation.

Truths about men and women.
About success and honor.

Not really, said Einstein with a twinkle
that could have been the detonation of an atom

in his bright brown eye.

XXXVIII. REVELATION

There must have been one early morning
with the bourbon worn off,
the girls ordered home,
the lackeys passed out
in corners and corridors;

there must have been that moment
with bed sheets twisted on the floor,
clothes shed like snakeskin,
rings off the fingers, Rolex from the wrist;

there must have been that time
with the planets aligned,
a comet flaring,
moonlight occupying the room
in its monthly hubris; that time

when the ceiling's mirror, unable
to escape or turn its eye, in a lapse
instantly regretted,
revealed the graven image within an image:
Emperor undressed, solipsistic nightmare,
icon of emptiness
for that second of pure revelation,

before the fist jabbed up
through the offending mirror
and on through the ceiling's plaster,
the floorboards,
the four poster bed of the nobody high-roller
dreaming of tomorrow's losses.

* * *

Of course the nobody recognized the fist –
of course he apologized in his broken-backed agonies
for existing in the space the fist entered:
Mr. Sinatra, this will never happen again.

Forget it pal, Frank muttered, snapping his fingers
for a bell hop with a dozen roses, long-stemmed,
his token of forgiveness.

XXXIX. PARABLE OF THE PRODIGAL SON

There was a man whose two sons lived with him, worked his land, tended his sheep. The father loved each, fed and cared for each, and kept each close.

One day the younger son asked his father for his share of property. And the father consented.

The younger son took all he had to a far country, where he squandered his wealth on harlots and drink. And when he'd spent everything, his friends told him to go home, but he would not.

A great famine arose in that country, and he found work from a farmer, who paid him to tend swine. And he fed on the pods the swine ate, and drank water from their trough, and lay in the stalls with them at night. Still he would not go home.

When no more work could be had, he wandered the roads, begging alms from passersby, then singing and dancing for pennies in the taverns.

And all who knew him counseled him to go home and beg forgiveness. But he would not go.

When the father heard of his son's condition, he ordered the elder son to find him, dress him in a fine robe, with a ring on his finger and good shoes on his feet. Then the fatted calf would be slaughtered and the family united.

* * *

When the brothers saw each other in the lowest tavern of the poorest city, they embraced and touched each other's faces, laughing as they never had before. And the younger son turned to the drunks and the harlots, shouting out:

"This is my brother, who was dead, and is now alive, who was lost, and now is found."

XL. ON THE DAY GRAVITY FAILED

It was in the doldrums of his career,
walking across the stage for yet another taped show,
one shoe stubbornly in front of the other, as usual,

the cameras and cue cards in place,
the studio audience preparing their hands
for the applause box, the orchestra
reaching its practiced crescendo,

when one foot without his consent
lifted and never touched down,
and the other rose higher than the first,

and he kept climbing into mid-air,
ascending an invisible staircase
with the audience applauding
each new step in the act.

That's when the two words found themselves
in his throat: *why not? why not?*
why not fly up and away
by flapping arms, kicking legs,
accepting the miracle
not for any *flying honeymoon*
but alone and silent and unrepentant.

But Frank, not seeing the odds
in his favor, eased himself out of the air
back onto the floor in front of the cameras,
the cue cards, the expectant faces,
the microphone, which he grasped as usual
with both hands and a sigh of relief,

* * *

as if a miracle is just another obstacle
to overcome.

XLI. SIX TRUTHS ABOUT MONEY

(1)

In truth, he created money before
he created men and women,
setting its core ablaze and placing it
on an altar in the Garden
so it might shine brighter than the sun.

(2)

In truth, money created itself,
moving its spirit over the face of the water,
organizing its forms out of neglected dust,
offering allegiance to no god or human
but finding its inevitable place
wherever two or three are gathered.

(3)

In truth, money was never created
but existed only in the stories
men and women told about it
as they tried to understand themselves,
and the objects their hands made,
and the objects their hands desired.

(4)

In truth, it was the stories about money
that created money, told so often
with such passion by so many
that no one could deny its existence
in their pockets, in their banks,
or in the banks of other people
who said few words,
and kept mostly to themselves.

(5)

In truth, money remade those who owned it
into taller and heavier beings
whose footsteps echoed
from mountain to mountain to mountain.

At the same time it created the machines
that make more money
and the ones that clean money,
the ones that hide it,
and the ones that take it away.

(6)

In truth, money first crawled on its belly
but complained so loudly about not being able to fly
that he gave it wings, talons, a beak.

With its beak, money dug a hole in the ground,
where it crawled, furled its wings,
tucked its talons,
and waited stubbornly for the end of time.

XLII. SEVEN PROVERBS

(1)

Boast about tomorrow,
for you cannot know
what today will bring.

(2)

It is better to cut your own throat
than let another man cut it for you.

(3)

Better is hidden love
than open rebuke.

(4)

Profuse are the kisses of a friend
but faithful
are the wounds of an enemy.

(5)

A wise man gives full vent to his anger;
a fool quietly holds it back.

(6)

The righteous flee when no one pursues,
but the wicked are bold as a lion.

(7)

Trouble makes the heart glad,
but oil and perfume tear the soul.

XLIII. FRANK IN HIS OWN COMPANY

Tired of the Jersey funhouse,
the ferris wheel grinding
its pointless arc;
wearied by carnies' t-shirts and darting eyes,
Frank seeks out the Hall of Mirrors,
where no tickets are torn,
no fake floors collapse –
only mirrors, remorseless light, silence,
the isolated self, replicated –
in case you don't get it the first time –
a thousand thousand times:
an army of Frank diminished
to a speck at the back
of the endless single file,
Frank in his own company
skittering along surfaces,
conforming to the convex and the concave,
accommodating warps, fissures, bends,
all the polished folds
of the secret self.

XLIV. RETIREMENT

When the prayers arrived Frank was confused:
What do you want from me?
He granted one petition, ignored another,
punished some for personal reasons
or an evening's irritability.
He never apologized.

In time, he grew dependent on their need:
they celebrated his indifference
as a kind of love, justified even
that unpredictable temper. In time,
he believed what they believed
he believed about the world he made.

Then came the denunciations
from street corners and pulpits.
Treatises on inconsistencies.
New gods to worship.
And he responded as of old:
What do you want from me?

And they jeered him and mocked him:
the hair transplants, the puffy face,
wives younger than their great-granddaughters.
Where, he bellowed from the microphone
that someone had unplugged long ago,
where is the love?

He withdrew to Palm Springs,
locked his gates, sulking,
singing only to himself
of the twilight years and lost love
and a universe of strangers in the night.

* * *

He's dead, some proclaimed, almost joyfully.
Others: *He never lived at all.*
And the remnant of his fans:
We loved him; we love him still.

XLV. STILL LIFE IN A PARK

Oh to be young! –
and not give a shit about you

or your friend
or the person next to your friend –

but instead lounge
beneath the immense statue
of what's-his-name

with the sun distant in the sky
like a woman
alone in her bedroom.

XLVI. THE CITY ACCORDING TO FRANK

Nothing like concrete and brick,
glass and steel, mouths waving,

arms shouting, to save the mind
from those open spaces, the infinite

possibilities, the uncomfortable green,
the still-breathing leaves. Nothing like

all those people so far away
on the streets, in subways,

on sidewalks, so many destinations
to save the mind from dwelling

on that master terminus
where every route leads.

XLVII. ESCHATOLOGY: FRANK AND ELVIS

One day each of us must turn from the microphone
to greet that hillbilly striding across the stage,
done up in black for the TV special.

This can't be real, we'll say
when he plants his feet so near,
half shuts those infamous eyelids,

grinds his hips to our orchestra's rhythms –
the rhythms we thought we owned –
and smirks for reasons

we can't understand,
eclipsing Vegas, defunct Dino
sloshing his highball, Sammy chucking

an irritated elbow,
all those tired hats at their rakish tilt
toward the chorus girls.

What can we do in that terrible moment
but shift our weight,
contrive a quick shuffle,

and gaze up and away
toward the far off lens and cue card
that cannot be ignored?

What can we do in the face
of this certain future
but extend a finger at the end of its snap

and smile, Frank, smile
that million-dollar smile?

NOTES

I. BIRTH IN HOBOKEN

"He was a scrapper from birth, so large—twelve and three-quarter pounds—that he had to be pulled out of his ninety-pound mother with medical forceps .... Delivered in the bedroom of the Sinatra apartment, the baby was at first pronounced stillborn and set aside by the doctor while he worked to save the life of the mother. But, as neighborhood women who had gathered around shrieked and wept, Dolly's mother plucked up the baby, carried him into the bathroom, and held him under the cold-water faucet. A moment later, Francis Albert Sinatra wailed for the first time." (Lew Irwin, *Sinatra: A Life Remembered*, Philadelphia: Courage Books, 1997)

"...I mean, we had a ukulele player, and we'd stand on the corner and sing songs." (Frank Sinatra, quoted in Lew Irwin's *Sinatra: A Life Remembered*)

III. YES, YES, YES, YES

Stories of the miraculous childhoods of certain heroic figures are common in the eighth-century Irish epic *Tain Bo Cuailnge* and the Welsh medieval tales of *The Mabinogi*.

IV. THE FIGHT

Sinatra's father, Anthony Martin Sinatra, was a boxer who fought under the name Marty O'Brien.

VII. THE GARDEN ACCORDING TO FRANK

A Place in the Sun: motto of the Sands Hotel, Las Vegas.

XV. THIS WAY

This poem draws from the story of the attempted murder of Lleu Llaw Gyffes in the Fourth Branch of *The Mabinogi*. The quotation is from John Bollard's translation, *The Mabinogi: Legend and Landscape of Wales* (Llandysul, Gomer Press: 2006).

XVI. THE HOUSE THAT FRANK BUILT

In the Second Branch of *The Mabinogi*, the head of Bendigeidfran is able to exist without its body and converse with friends for 87 years.

XVIII. UNLEASHED

Arawn, Lord of the Underworld, appears with a pack of hounds when Pwyll and he first meet in the First Branch of *The Mabinogi*.

XX. UNCREATION

The communication between the bird and Frank draws from the Second Branch of *The Mabinogi*.

XXI. WARP-SPASM

Warp-Spasm: the frenzy that Cuchulain, hero of the *Tain Bo Cuailnge*, experiences before battle.

Gossip columnist Louella Parsons reported that Peter Lawford had been spotted at a Beverly Hills restaurant having drinks with Ava Gardner. (Lew Irwin's *Sinatra: A Life Remembered*)

XXXI. VISITING BOGIE

"[Frank Sinatra] regularly visited Humphrey Bogart in the hospital, often accompanied by other members of the Pack, all doing their best to keep the good-time goals of the group intact." (Lew Irwin's *Sinatra: A Life Remembered*)

How's your bird?: "'Bird' was the male organ, and the term was constantly used as a jovial greeting, as in, 'How's your bird?'" (Lew Irwin's *Sinatra: A Life Remembered*)

XXXIII. DREAM AT SUNRISE

Uncle Babe, Champ Sieger: Sinatra's uncles.

XXXV. READING EMILY DICKINSON

Arthur Miller and Marilyn Monroe were married from 1956 to 1961. Thomas Johnson's definitive edition of Emily Dickinson's *Collected Poems* appeared in 1955.

XLVII. ESCHATOLOGY: FRANK AND ELVIS

Frank Sinatra hosted Elvis Presley on his April 1960 TV Special for ABC—the only time the two performed together.

DAVID LLOYD was born in Utica, New York, and grew up in the Welsh community there. A graduate of St. Lawrence University, Lloyd received his MA in Creative Writing and his Ph.D. in literature from Brown University. He now directs the Creative Writing Program at Le Moyne College. In 2000, he received the Poetry Society of America's Robert H. Winner Memorial Award. His articles, interviews, poems, and stories have appeared in magazines in the US, Canada, and Britain, including *Crab Orchard Review*, *Denver Quarterly*, *DoubleTake*, *Planet*, *Poetry Wales*, and *TriQuarterly*. He is the editor of *The Urgency of Identity: Contemporary English-language Poetry from Wales* and the author of *Writing on the Edge: Interviews with Writers and Editors of Wales*. His poetry collection *The Everyday Apocalypse*, published by Three Conditions Press, won the 2002 Maryland State Poetry & Literary Society's chapbook contest. His fiction collection, *Boys: Stories and a Novella*, was published by Syracuse University Press in 2004, and his anthology *Other Land: Contemporary Poems on Wales and Welsh-American Experience* appeared from Parthian Books in 2008. He served as poetry editor for *DoubleTake/Points of Entry* and as fiction editor for the 2008 issue of *Stone Canoe*. He lives in Manlius, New York, with his wife, artist Kim Waale, and their daughter.

www.ingramcontent.com/pod-product-compliance
Lightning Source LLC
Chambersburg PA
CBHW051709040426
42446CB00008B/791